BOOKKEEPING AND ACCOUNTING

ESSENTIALS

FOR SMALL BUSINESS OWNERS

Practicum Press

© 2020 by Antony P. Ng

No part of this publication may be reproduced or distributed in any form or by any means, electronic or mechanical, without written permission from the author or the publisher.

Practicum Press
Austin, Texas

Printed in the United States of America

ISBN: 978-1-0762735-6-7

For my grandmother who always believed in me
and from whom I learned what love is.

Disclaimer

This book is for informational purposes only. This book does not provide legal advice, and should not be substituted for advice from accountants and legal professionals. Neither the author nor the publisher guarantees or warrants that the information in this book is accurate, complete or up-to-date.

Acknowledgments

I would like to thank Lisa Tatum, Emily Chiu, Kathleen Hausenfluck, Nikhila Janamanchi and Sara Foskitt for their time and effort in reading the manuscript as well as adding valuable insights.

Forward

Just fresh out of real estate schools, many real estate agents quickly dive into consulting and selling. Suffice to say, many of them are good salespersons and can earn themselves very high revenues in terms of commissions. But the feeling of accomplishment fades away quickly once they realize that a substantial amount of their hard-earned revenue is lost to business expenses and income taxes. This is usually a turning point for many rookie agents. They begin to realize selling is only part of a successful real estate career, learning how to keep what they have earned is the other part.

Because an accounting course is typically not part of the real estate licensing programs, many real estate agents have to learn how to keep track of business expenses on their own. Some real estate agents rely on their accountant to keep track of their business, but who knows your business better than you? Thus, it is beneficial for real estate agents to learn the financial side of their real estate business.

As a real estate broker, I am excited to see a book that teaches basic bookkeeping and accounting. This book takes us back to the very basics of accounting. By basics, I mean the very first debit/credit entries we learned ever so long ago in college. It literally goes over everything a real estate agent needs to know about the proper way of recording business expenses, depreciation and amortization, payroll, etc. Importantly, the book teaches a real estate agent how to analyze profitability of his/her real estate business. If taken to heart, such information will help you grow your real estate business and increase your profits simply by making the right financial decisions. Smart business owners know how well their companies are doing at any given moment and are able to adjust to industry changes instantly, so this is exactly what we all need!

Beata Burgeson, Broker Associate, CRS, GRI, ABR, CNE
Kuper Sotheby's International Realty

TABLE OF CONTENTS

Introduction 1

PART I
BOOKKEEPING

CHAPTER 1   DEFINITIONS 7

CHAPTER 2   RECORDING TRANSACTIONS 13
                    Transactions 13
                    Accounting Methods 14
                    Bookkeeping Methods 18

CHAPTER 3   SINGLE-ENTRY METHOD 21
                    Revenue & Expense Journal 21
                    Example of Single-entry method 24

CHAPTER 4   DOUBLE-ENTRY METHOD 27
                    Chart of Accounts 27
                    General Journal 29
                    Example of Double-entry method 30
                    General Ledger 35

CHAPTER 5   OTHER BUSINESS RECORDS 39
                    Accounts Receivable 39
                    Accounts Payable 40
                    Fixed Assets Log 41
                    Travel & Entertainment Log 41
                    Payroll Register 42

PART II
ACCOUNTING

CHAPTER 6	ACCOUNTING AUTHORITIES	45
	Financial Accounting Foundation	45
	Generally Accepted Accounting Principles	45
	International Financial Reporting Standards	46
CHAPTER 7	FINANCIAL STATEMENTS	47
	Income Statement	48
	Balance Sheet	50
	Cash Flow Statement	51
	Statement of Retained Earnings	53
CHAPTER 8	FINANCIAL ANALYSIS	55
	Profitability Ratios	55
	Liquidity Ratios	58
	Expense Analysis	60

PART III
BUSINESS-RELATED TOPICS

CHAPTER 9 BUSINESS ENTITIES 63
    Types of business entities 63
    Register the selected business entity 65
    Obtain an Employer Identification Number 66

CHAPTER 10 PAYROLL TAXES 67
    Social Security and Medicare Taxes 67
    Unemployment Tax 68

CHAPTER 11 ALLOCATING PROFITS 71
    Divide Expenses Equally 72
    Divide Expenses Proportionally 72
    Divide Expenses Exactly 73

CHAPTER 12 DEPRECIATION AND AMORTIZATION 75
    Depreciation of Tangible Assets 75
    Amortization of Intangible Assets 76

GLOSSARY 77

Introduction

Many people tend to associate accounting with paying taxes, even though it is not what accounting is all about. There are many reasons for business owners to learn the concepts of bookkeeping and accounting even if the business owners are not planning to do the bookkeeping and accounting themselves.

The first, and probably the most important, reason is to know how the business is doing on a regular basis. Since business owners earn profits, bookkeeping and accounting are the ways for them to figure out how much profits their businesses have made. No accountant can magically figure out the profit numbers for a business owner if no one keeps track of the financial numbers that determine the profits.

Some business owners talk about taking a "salary" from their business, but unless their business structure allows them to do so, business owners generally do NOT receive a salary. If there is no salary, then how can a business owner pay for essential stuff to live? The answer is that the business owner takes a draw or distribution from the profit of the business; that is, when the business has made a profit. This means a business owner needs to know what the profit numbers are.

The second reason is to help business owners to communicate better with their bookkeeper and/or accountant. Even if the business owners have bookkeepers and/or accountants to do bookkeeping and accounting for them, it would be beneficial for the business owners to have a general understanding on what their bookkeepers and/or accountants are doing, and to give them directions when necessary.

The third reason is for business owners to figure out how much estimate tax they need to pay the Internal Revenue Service (IRS) each quarter. Since most business owners do not receive a salary with tax already taken out from their paychecks, they are still require to pay an estimate tax to the IRS on a quarterly basis based on their profits made in the previous quarter.

The purpose of this book is to provide a general framework for small business owners who want to be more familiar with the bookkeeping and accounting processes. This book is not intended to be a treatise on bookkeeping and accounting, but rather a guide on various essential bookkeeping and accounting concepts.

Part I of this book explains the methods of bookkeeping. Many examples are presented to illustrate what information needs to be recorded for bookkeeping purpose. Part II of this book deals with the principles of accounting. They allow business owners to analyze the health of their business based on the information recorded through bookkeeping. Part III of this book provides additional business-related topics that should be helpful to many business owners.

PART I

BOOKKEEPING

Chapter 1

Definitions

Bookkeeping

Bookkeeping is the process of recording business transactions. Bookkeeping establishes the foundation for accounting.

Accounting

Accounting is the process of preparing financial statements by summarizing the business transactions recorded through bookkeeping. Accounting also includes analyzing and reporting financial information in a manner that facilitates business decision making.

Revenues

Revenues are all monies earned by a business in any given period of time. Revenues can be derived from sales of goods, sales of services, interest, and any miscellaneous sources.

However, capital deposits are not revenues. Also, monies from loans are not to be considered as revenues either.

Expenses

Expenses are all monies spent by a business. Operating expenses are expenses directly related to the normal operation of a business, which include rents, salaries, supplies, etc. Operating expenses tend to be recurring.

Non-operating expenses are expenses not related to the normal operation of a business. As such, non-operating expenses are usually not recurring. One example of non-operating expenses would be settlement cost of a lawsuit.

Some examples of business expenses are as follows:

Advertising	Parking Fees
Bad Debts	Postage
Bank Charges	Professional Services
Commissions	Rent
Contract Services	Repairs
Dues	Salaries
Equipment	Subscriptions
Food	Taxes
Insurance	Telephone/Internet
Legal Fees	Tools
License Fees	Utilities
Loan Interest	Uniforms
Office Supplies	Vehicle Expenses

Deductible Expenses

Under the Internal Revenue Code, certain business expenses (both operating and non-operating expenses) are considered as tax *deductible expenses*. Many business expenses are deductible in their entirety in the fiscal year[1] in which they are incurred. It would be beneficial for business owners to familiarize themselves with tax deductible expenses

Profits

After ascertaining the total amount of revenues and the total amount of expenses, *profit*[2] can be calculated via a profit equation as follows:

$$\text{Profit} = \text{Revenues} - \text{Expenses}$$

The main goal of many businesses is to make profits. It is clear from the profit equation that profit can be increased by increasing revenues and/or reducing expenses.

Depreciable assets

Instead of deductible in their entirety in the year in which they are incurred, the expenses on certain business assets, such as business properties, production machinery, office furniture, vehicles, etc., need to be deducted over multiple years. This group of assets is known as *depreciable assets*. The method for deducting the costs of depreciable assets over multiple years is known as *depreciation* (*see* Chapter 12).

---

[1] A fiscal year is any twelve-month accounting period. A fiscal year can, but is not required to, be coincide with the calendar year.

[2] Also known as net income.

Section 179 deduction

Under § 179 of the Internal Revenue Code, when a depreciable asset is qualified as a *qualifying property*, a business is allowed to treat all or part of the cost of the depreciable asset as an expense completely deductible in the year in which it is incurred, instead of over multiple years.

Assets, Liabilities and Equity

The financial condition of a business can be expressed by the relationship of *assets* to *liabilities* and *owner's equity*.

Assets are all properties owned by a business. Assets include current assets and long-term assets. Current assets are items that can be converted into cash within one year or less, such as cash-in-bank and account receivable. Long-term assets are any assets that are not considered as current assets, such property and equipment.

Liabilities are all debts the business currently has outstanding to creditors. Liabilities include current liabilities and long-term liabilities. Current liabilities are debts that need to be paid off within one year or less, such as account payable. Long-term liabilities are any liabilities that are not considered as current liabilities.

Owner's Equity is the interest of an owner in the business. Owner's equity may include capital and retained earnings.

Accounting Equation

Assets, liabilities and owner's equity are related to each other via a fundamental equation known as the *accounting equation*. The accounting equation states that, without exceptions, the following relationship must always be true:

$$\text{Assets} = \text{Liabilities} + \text{Owner's Equity}$$

According to the accounting equation, a business is assumed to possess its assets subject to the rights of its creditors and owners.

For example, when a business owns assets of $200,000, owes creditors $120,000, and owes the business owner $80,000, the accounting equation looks like:

$$200{,}000 = 120{,}000 + 80{,}000$$
$$\text{Assets} \quad \text{Liabilities} \quad \text{Owner's Equity}$$

After a period of time, when the business pays off $15,000 of the debt, the liabilities are reduced by $15,000. If the assets are not changed, the owner's equity is increased by $15,000, and the accounting equation becomes:

$$200{,}000 = 105{,}000 + 95{,}000$$
$$\text{Assets} \quad \text{Liabilities} \quad \text{Owner's Equity}$$

Transaction

A *transaction* is any business event that alters the amount of assets, liabilities and/or owner's equity.

Journalizing

Every transaction must be recorded as an entry in a journal in chronological order, and the process is called *journalizing*.

CHAPTER 2

RECORDING TRANSACTIONS

Transactions

For any business, many transactions can typically occur in one day. The following is an example of the various transactions took place during January 2018 for a small company:

DATE	TRANSACTIONS
1	Issued Check 2100 for $1,100 to pay rent.
5	Performed services for $2,200 in cash.
6	Performed services for $2,900 on credit.
10	Paid $200 for monthly telephone bill with Check 2101.
11	Paid $150 for equipment repairs with Check 2102.
15	Issued Check 2103 for $200 to purchase new equipment.
18	Issued Check 2104 for $250 to purchase office supplies.
22	Performed services for $2,900 in cash.
23	Performed services for $3,500 on credit.
28	Issued Check 2105 for $280 to purchase office supplies.
31	Paid monthly electric bill of $270 with Check 2106.

The exact transaction depends on the type of business, but for the most part, transactions are either about collecting money (*i.e.*, revenues) or about spending money (*i.e.*, expenses). Each of the transactions needs to be recorded accordingly. For accurate reflections of money collected and spent, it is important not to commingle expenses with revenues by simply recording the difference between revenue and expense. Thus, revenue transactions need to be recorded separately from expense transactions.

Accounting Methods

There are two accounting methods (or accounting basis) for recording transactions:

    i.   cash basis
    ii.   accrual basis

Cash basis

With the cash basis of accounting, revenues are recorded under the date when monies are received, and expenses are recorded under the date when monies are sent out. Many small businesses prefer to use the cash basis of accounting because it is simple and intuitive. One major drawback with the cash basis of accounting is that, while reflecting the business' cash in hand, it does not always reflect other economic realities of the business.

Accrual basis

With the accrual basis of accounting, revenues are recorded under the date goods are delivered and/or services are provided, regardless of when monies are received. Similarly, expenses are recognized under the date goods and/or services are received, regardless of when the business actually pays for the goods and/or services.

The goal of the accrual basis of accounting is to eliminate the major shortcoming of the cash method of accounting, *i.e.*, distortions of economic reality due to the time lag between when goods/services are delivered/provided and when payments for the goods/services.

The following are two transaction examples illustrating the difference between the Cash basis and Accrual basis of accounting.

Example 1: Service Revenue Transaction

DATE	TRANSACTIONS
Jan 15	company sent an invoice of $5,000 to customer for services rendered
Feb 5	customer paid the $5,000 invoice

Cash basis

On January 15, no record entry is required because there is no money exchange between the company and the customer. On February 5, the receipt of $5,000 payment is recorded by the company, and the $5,000 payment is reflected as February revenue.

Accrual basis

On January 15, the receipt of $5,000 payment is recorded by the company even though no money has been exchanged, and the $5,000 payment is reflected as January revenue. The payment is considered to have been earned by the company on January 15 (*i.e.*, the invoice date), even though the company will not receive payment until February 5.

Example 2: Goods Expense Transaction

DATE	TRANSACTIONS
Jan 25	company purchased $250 worth of office supplies from Office Depot
Jan 31	Office Depot sent company an invoice
Feb 10	company paid the $250 invoice

Cash basis

On January 25, no record entry is made by the company because there is no money exchange between the company and Office Depot. On February 10, the $250 payment is recorded by the company as an expense, and the $250 payment is reflected as a February expense.

Accrual basis

On January 25, the $250 payment is recorded by the company as an expense even though no money has been exchanged, and the $250 payment is reflected as a January expense. The company is considered to have incurred the $250 expense on January 25 (*i.e.*, the purchase date), even though the company will not pay for the office supply until February 10.

How to change Accounting Method

A change in accounting method includes a change in:

1. overall method, such as from cash to accrual or *vice versa*; and
2. treatment of any material item.

Once a business has chosen its accounting method on its initial income tax filing, the business must seek approval from the Internal Revenue Service before it can change to a different accounting method.

Seeking an approval from the Internal Revenue Service to change an accounting method can be performed under either the automatic change procedure or the advance consent request procedure. Generally, a Form 3115 (Application for Change in Accounting Method) must be filed with the Internal Revenue Service in order to request an automatic change.

If a taxpayer complies with the provisions of the automatic change procedure, the approval is granted for the tax year for which the taxpayer requests a change (year of change). No user fee is required for an application filed under an automatic change procedure generally covered in Revenue Procedure 2002-9.

Bookkeeping Methods

There are two bookkeeping methods for recording transactions:

i. single-entry method
ii. double-entry method

Single-entry method

Single-entry method is a simple bookkeeping procedure that primarily uses Revenue and Expense information. The main requirement is the usage of a Revenue & Expense journal for chronicling daily transactions such as receipts and expenditures. Details of single-entry method can be found in Chapter 3.

The concept of single-entry method is relatively straight-forward and is much easier to understand for beginners than double-entry method.

Double-entry method

Double-entry method is based on the premise that the accounting equation (from Chapter 1) must always be observed when journalizing each transaction.

Double-entry method requires every transaction to be recorded as *debits* and *credits* in a general journal—the book of original entry. The terms debit and credit simply refer to the left and right sides of an amount column, respectively. It is important to remember that in bookkeeping vernacular, the terms debit and credit do not have the common non-accounting connotation. The two halves of a double-entry always have to be equal, *i.e.*, the debits side always equals the credits side for every transaction. Details of double-entry method can be found in Chapter 4.

Tips

1. Cash method of accounting
    - ♦ record revenue when money is received
    - ♦ record expense when an expense is paid

    Advantage: accurately shows how much cash are available
    Disadvantage: does not provide an accurate flow of revenue and debts

2. Accrual method of accounting
    - ♦ record revenue when an invoice is sent for services rendered or goods delivered
    - ♦ record expense when an invoice is received for services/goods received

    Advantage: accurately shows the flow of revenue and debts
    Disadvantage: does not show how much cash reserves are available

3. Businesses having sales less than $5 million per year are free to choose either cash method or accrual method of accounting, but most small businesses use cash method of accounting.

4. Internal Revenue Service requires a business to use accrual method of accounting when the business has an inventory of items to be sold to public.

Chapter 3

Single-entry Method

With the single-entry method of bookkeeping, the flow of accounting data can be illustrated as follows:

TRANSACTION → an entry in REVENUE & EXPENSE JOURNAL

A Revenue & Expense Journal is utilized to record all transactions. After a transaction has been completed, the information shown on a business document, such as an invoice or receipt, which substantiates the completed transaction is then added as a new entry in the Revenue & Expense Journal. Transactions should be entered in the Revenue & Expense Journal in chronological order according to the dates provided on the corresponding business documents.

Single-entry method allows record keeping of all transactions to be accomplished by simply entering revenues and expenses in one Revenue & Expense Journal.

Revenue & Expense Journal

Each page of a Revenue & Expense journal should be assigned with various column headings to cover all major categories of revenues and expenses. Subsequently, each transaction is recorded as a revenue or expense.

Most transactions for which monies are received can be recorded as revenues. But equity or capital deposits and monies from loans are not revenues. Most transactions for which monies are paid out can be recorded as expenses. But owner draws and principal payments on loans are not expenses.

A page of a Revenue & Expense journal should look like this:

Revenue & Expense Journal

DATE	CHECK NO.	TRANSACTION	REVENUE	EXPENSE	Business dependent	MISC.
		TOTALS				

Common Column Headings

For any business, the first five column headings in a Revenue & Expense journal typically are:

1. Date
2. Check Number
3. Transaction
4. Revenue
5. Expense

Business-dependent Column Headings

The next group of column headings are used for identifying individual categories of revenue from which monies are frequently received and expense on which checks are frequently written. This group of column headings varies from business to business.

For example, such column headings for a law firm may include revenue categories such as legal services and interest, and expense categories such as advertising, insurance, rent and salaries.

Miscellaneous and Totals

The last column heading in a Revenue & Expense journal should be Miscellaneous. The Miscellaneous column heading serves as a catch-all for any expense that does not fall under any other column heading. For example, license fee is paid only once a year, so it does not warrant a "license fee" column heading. Thus, the payment of license fee should be first recorded under the Expense column, and then under the Miscellaneous column, along with an explanation either under the Transaction column or in parentheses next to the amount in the Miscellaneous column. The explanation allows infrequent expenses to be grouped under one column and still be able to allocate them to appropriate expenses categories when preparing an Income Statement (*see* Chapter 7).

Each of the Revenue and Expense columns should have a total at the bottom of a Journal page. All totals are then transferred to the top of a next Journal page and accumulated until the end of a month. At the end of each month, the last Journal page is totaled. This is known as *closing entries*[3] for the month. After closing entries, certain entries need to be reconciled with a bank statement, much like a check book register, in order to ensure the month's entries are recorded accurately.

A new month begins with a clean Journal page with all zero balances.

---

[3] Closing entries are also performed at the end of a fiscal year.

Example of Single-entry method

The following is an example of recording transactions in a Revenue & Expense journal using the single-entry method under cash basis for the month of March. Every single transaction has one entry in the Revenue & Expense journal.

DATE	TRANSACTIONS
Mar 1	a business owner started a new company by depositing $20,000 capital in an operating account at a bank
Mar 2	company purchased $500 worth of office supplies with check 1001
Mar 5	company purchases $10,000 worth of office furniture by making a down payment of $2,000 with check 1002 and by financing the balance with a loan of $8,000
Mar 10	company invoiced a client $5,000 for service rendered (invoice 101)
Mar 31	company received $5,000 payment for invoice 101 from client

The entries to the Revenue & Expense journal for the above-mentioned transactions using cash basis of accounting are as follows:

DATE	CHECK NO.	TRANSACTION	REVENUE	EXPENSE	...	MISC.
Mar 1		capital deposit				$20,000
Mar 2	1001	office supplies		$500		
Mar 5	1002	office furniture		$2,000		
Mar 31		service rendered	$5,000			invoice 101
		TOTALS	$5,000	$2,500		

For the Mar 5 entry, in addition to the expense entry in the Revenue & Expense journal, the $8,000 loan for purchasing office furniture is recorded in an Account Payable journal, and the office furniture is recorded in a Fixed Assets Log (*see* Chapter 5).

Note that there is no entry in the Revenue & Expense journal for the Mar 10 transaction under the cash basis of accounting because no cash was exchanged.

CHAPTER 4

DOUBLE-ENTRY METHOD

With the double-entry method of bookkeeping, the flow of accounting data can be illustrated as follows:

TRANSACTION → credit/debit entries in GENERAL JOURNAL

After a transaction has been completed, the information shown on a business document, such as an invoice or a receipt, that substantiates the completed transaction is then posted to at least two appropriate offsetting accounts as credit(s) and debit(s). Thus, the double-entry method requires the initial setting up of accounts for each category of assets, liabilities, equity, revenues and expenses, where all of these accounts are collectively referred to as the *Chart of Accounts*. Transactions should be entered in the appropriate accounts in chronological order according to the dates provided on the corresponding business documents.

Chart of Accounts

As note above, all the accounts can generally be grouped under the following five major categories:

- Assets
- Liabilities
- Equity
- Revenues
- Expenses

Basically, each category contains its own individual accounts, and each of the accounts may be further divided into various subaccounts, if necessary. The accounts in the Assets, Liabilities and Equity categories are considered as balance sheet accounts because they contribute information to the corresponding sections of a Balance Sheet (*see* Chapter 7). Similarly, the accounts in the Revenues and Expenses categories are considered as income statement accounts because they contribute information to the corresponding sections of an Income Statement (*see* Chapter 7).

The Chart of Accounts should correspond to the type of business. For example, the Chart of Accounts for a law firm may look like:

Assets
Cash in Bank
Accounts Receivable
Prepaid Expenses
Fixed Assets
Accumulated Depreciation

Liabilities
Accounts Payable
Loan Payable
Taxes Payable

Equity
Owner's Capital
Retained Profits

Revenues
Legal Services
Interest

Expenses
Accounting
Advertising
Office Furniture
Office Supplies
Insurance
Licenses
Rent
Salaries
Taxes
Travel

General Journal

A general journal is utilized to record every transaction as debits and credits. An example of a general journal is shown as follows:

General Journal

Date	Entries	Debits	Credits

In the accounting world, "debit" and "credit" simply refer to the left and right sides of an amount column, respectively, of a general journal. Under the double-entry method, for each transaction, typically two entries need to be made in a general journal, one on the debits side and one on the credits side of an amount column.

The standard debits/credits entry rule is that Assets (*i.e.*, the left side of the Accounting Equation) are increased with debits, and decreased with credits, while the Liabilities and Equity (*i.e.*, the right side of the Accounting Equation) are increased with credits, and decrease with debits.

The debits/credits journal entry rule can be summarized in Table I:

Debit	Credit
Assets increase	Assets decrease
Expenses increase	Expenses decrease
Liabilities decrease	Liabilities increase
Equity decreases	Equity increases
Revenues decrease	Revenues increase

Table I

Basically, a first entry is made on the debits side when there is an increase in an Assets account or a decrease in a Liabilities or Equity account. Also, a first entry can be made on the debits side when there is a decrease in a Revenues account (which is similar to a decrease in the Equity account). Next, a second entry is made on the credits side when there is a decrease in an Assets account or an increase in a Liabilities or Equity account. Also, a second entry can be made in the credits side when there is an increase in a Revenues account (which is similar to an increase in the Equity account). Thus, for each double-entry, the amount in debits side is always equal the amount in the credits side. By using the double-entry method, the Accounting Equation always stays in balance after each transaction is recorded since both sides of the Accounting Equation are increased or decreased by the same amount.

Examples of Double-entry method

The following are examples of recording transactions in a general journal using the double-entry credits/debits journal entry rules under the cash basis method. The transactions are the same as the transaction example in Chapter 3 illustrating the single-entry method.

DATE	TRANSACTIONS
Mar 1	a business owner started a new company by depositing $20,000 capital in an operating account at a bank
Mar 2	company purchased $500 worth of office supplies with check 1001
Mar 5	company purchases $10,000 worth of office furniture by making a down payment of $2,000 with check 1002 and by financing the balance with a loan of $8,000
Mar 10	company invoiced a client $5,000 for service rendered (invoice 101)
Mar 31	company received $5,000 payment for invoice 101 from client

Every single transaction has at least one entry in the credits column and at least one entry in the debits column.

DATE   TRANSACTIONS
Mar 1   a business owner started a new company by depositing $20,000 capital in an operating account at a bank

This transaction affects two accounts, namely, the Asset account and the Equity account. The Asset account is affected because of an increase in Asset (cash-in-bank), and the Equity account is affected because of an increase in Equity (owner's capital).

CHARTS OF ACCOUNTS

Assets
- Cash in Bank ←
- Accounts Receivable
- Prepaid Expenses
- Fixed Assets

Liabilities
- Accounts Payable
- Loan Payable
- Taxes Payable

Equity
- Owner's Capital ←
- Retained Profits

Revenues
- Commissions
- Interest

Expenses
- Accounting
- Advertising
- Office Furniture
- Office Supplies
- Insurance
- Licenses
- Rent
- Salaries
- Taxes
- Travel

JOURNAL ENTRY RULES

Debit	Credit
Revenues decrease	Revenues increase
Expenses increase	Expenses decrease
Assets increase ←	Assets decrease
Liabilities decrease	Liabilities increase
Equity decreases	Equity increases ←

Referring to Journal Entry Rules (Table I), since the Asset (cash-in-bank account) is increased, an entry is recorded in the debits column, and since the Equity (business owner's capital) is also increased, an entry is recorded in the credits column. Thus, the correct double-entry for this transaction should be as follows:

Date	Entries	Debits	Credits
Mar 1	Cash in Bank	$20,000	
	Owner's Capital		$20,000

DATE   TRANSACTIONS

Mar 2   company purchased $500 worth of office supplies with a check

This transaction affects two accounts, namely, the Expense account and the Asset account. The Expense account is affected because of an increase in Expense (Office Supplies), and the Asset account is affected because of a decrease in Assets (Cash in Bank).

CHARTS OF ACCOUNTS

Assets
- Cash in Bank
- Accounts Receivable
- Prepaid Expenses
- Fixed Assets

Liabilities
- Accounts Payable
- Loan Payable
- Taxes Payable

Equity
- Owner's Capital
- Retained Profits

Revenues
- Commissions
- Interest

Expenses
- Accounting
- Advertising
- Office Furniture
- Office Supplies
- Insurance
- Licenses
- Rent
- Salaries
- Taxes
- Travel

JOURNAL ENTRY RULES

Debit	Credit
Revenues decrease	Revenues increase
Expenses increase	Expenses decrease
Assets increase	Assets decrease
Liabilities decrease	Liabilities increase
Equity decreases	Equity increases

Referring to Journal Entry Rules (Table I), since the Expense (office supplies account) is increased, an entry is recorded in the debits column, and since the Asset (cash-in-bank account) is decreased, an entry is recorded in the credits column. Thus, the correct double-entry for this transaction should be as follows:

Date	Entries	Debits	Credits
Mar 2	Office Supplies	$500	
	Cash in Bank		$500

DATE   TRANSACTIONS

Mar 5   company purchased $10,000 worth of office furniture by making a down payment of $2,000 with a check and by financing the balance with a loan of $8,000

This transaction affects three accounts, namely, the Asset account, the Expense account and the Liability account. The Asset account is affected because of an increase in Asset (cash-in-bank). The Expense account is affected because of an increase in Expense (Office Furniture), and the Liability account is affected because of an increase in Liability (debt).

CHARTS OF ACCOUNTS

Assets
Cash in Bank ←
Accounts Receivable
Prepaid Expenses
Fixed Assets

Liabilities
Accounts Payable
Loan Payable ←
Taxes Payable

Equity
Owner's Capital
Retained Profits

Revenues
Commissions
Interest

Expenses
Accounting
Advertising
Office Furniture
→ Office Supplies
Insurance
Licenses
Rent
Salaries
Taxes
Travel

JOURNAL ENTRY RULES

Debit	Credit
Revenues decrease	Revenues increase
Expenses increase ←	Expenses decrease
Assets increase	Assets decrease ←
Liabilities decrease	Liabilities increase ←
Equity decreases	Equity increases

Referring to Journal Entry Rules (Table I), since the Expense (office furniture account) is increased, an entry is recorded in the debits column. Since the Liability (loan payable account) is also increased, an entry is recorded in the credits column. Since the Asset (cash-in-bank account) is decreased, an entry is recorded in the credits column. Thus, the correct double-entry for this transaction should be as follows:

Date	Entries	Debits	Credit
Mar 5	Office Furniture	$10,000	
	Loan Payable		$8,000
	Cash in bank		$2,000

DATE	TRANSACTIONS
Mar 31	company received $5,000 payment from client

This transaction will affect two accounts, namely, the Asset account and the Revenue account. The Asset account is affected because of an increase in Expense (cash-in-bank account), and the Revenue account is affected because of an increase in Revenue (commissions account).

CHARTS OF ACCOUNTS

Assets
- Cash in Bank ←
- Accounts Receivable
- Prepaid Expenses
- Fixed Assets

Liabilities
- Accounts Payable
- Loan Payable
- Taxes Payable

Equity
- Owner's Capital
- Retained Profits

Revenues
- → Commissions
- Interest

Expenses
- Accounting
- Advertising
- Office Furniture
- Office Supplies
- Insurance
- Licenses
- Rent
- Salaries
- Taxes
- Travel

JOURNAL ENTRY RULES

Debit	Credit
Revenues decrease	Revenues increase ←
Expenses increase	Expenses decrease
Assets increase ←	Assets decrease
Liabilities decrease	Liabilities increase
Equity decreases	Equity increases

Referring to Journal Entry Rules (Table I), since the Asset (cash-in-bank account) has been increased, an entry is recorded in the debits column, and since the Revenue (commissions account) has been increased, an entry is recorded in the credits column. The correct double-entry for this transaction should be as follows:

Date	Entries	Debits	Credits
Mar 31	Cash in Bank	$5,000	
	Service		$5,000

General Ledger

The data in the general journal are subsequently transferred to individual account pages of a general ledger—the book of secondary entry, and the process is called *posting*.

A general ledger contains a record of each account. At least one page of the general ledger is assigned to an account recorded in the general journal. Thus, each entry in the general journal can be posted to a corresponding page or pages of the general ledger. For example, after posting all cash-in-bank entries from the above-mentioned example transactions 1-4, the cash account page, which is typically the first page, in the general ledger will look like:

CASH					
Date	Comments	Debit Amount	Date	Comments	Credit Amount
Mar 1		$20,000			
			Mar 2		$500
			Mar 5		$2,000
May 2		$5,000			

The total of the debit side is $25,000, and the total of the credit side is $2,500. Thus, the cash account has a debit balance of $25,000 - $2,500 = $22,500. Since an increase in Asset is recorded in the debit side, this positive balance of $22,500 on the debit side of the cash account means there is $22,500 in the bank.

After all the entries from the general journal have been posted to the various pages of the general ledger, a *trial balance* can be prepared to make sure all the entries had recorded correctly in both the general journal and the general ledger. A trial balance for the entries from the above-mentioned transaction examples will look like:

Trial Balance
(Before Adjusting and Closing Entries)

	Debits	Credits
Cash	22,500	
Services		5,000
Office Supplies	500	
Office Furniture	10,000	
Loan		8,000
Owner's Capital		20,000
Total	33,000	33,000

Since the debits column total equals the credits column total, all the entries in the general journal and the general ledger were recorded correctly.

Tips

1. With the double-entry method of bookkeeping, each transaction has at least two entries—debit and credit.

2. Debits mean left column and credits mean right column.

3. Always list the account that will be debited first (left column), and then the account that will be credited (right column).

4. For each transaction, make sure the total of debit equals the total of credit.

CHAPTER 5

OTHER BUSINESS RECORDS

As a good business practice, additional business records, also known as General records, are needed to keep track assets and other pertinent information. For any given business, the most common records include:

1. Accounts Receivable
2. Accounts Payable
3. Fixed Assets Log
4. Travel & Entertainment Log
5. Payroll Records
6. Customer Records
7. Independent Contractor Records

Accounts Receivable

An Accounts Receivable Record is used to keep track of money owed to a business as a result of extending credit to a client or customer who has acquired products and/or services. As such, a cash-only business generally does not need to keep an Accounts Receivable Record. Otherwise, it is important to have detailed information about the transactions and the balance owed for each invoice. This is accomplished by setting up a separate account record for each client or customer.

A page of an Account Receivable Record may look like:

Accounts Receivable

CLIENT: _____   ADDRESS: _____
TEL. NO: _____   ACCOUNT NO. _____

INVOICE DATE	INVOICE NUMBER	INVOICE AMOUNT	TERMS	DATE PAID	AMOUNT PAID	INVOICE BALANCE

Accounts Payable

Accounts payable are debts owned by a business to its creditors for goods purchased and/or services received. It is important to keep track of what a business owes and when it should pay in order to maintain a good credit record for the business. Accounts payable is not required for businesses that always pay their invoices in full and on time.

A page of an Account Payable Record may look like:

Accounts Payable

CREDITOR: _____   ADDRESS: _____
TEL. NO: _____   ACCOUNT NO. _____

INVOICE DATE	INVOICE NUMBER	INVOICE AMOUNT	TERMS	DATE PAID	AMOUNT PAID	INVOICE BALANCE

Fixed Assets Log

A Fixed Assets Log is used to keep an inventory of depreciable assets purchased during a tax year. The information from the fixed assets log can be utilized to prepare any allowable depreciation for the tax year (*see* Chapter 12).

A page of a Fixed Assets Log may look like:

Fixed Assets Log

ASSET	DATE PLACED IN SERVICE	COST OF ASSET	% USED FOR BUSINESS	RECOVERY PERIOD	METHOD OF DEPRECIATION	DATE SOLD	SALE PRICE

Travel & Entertainment Log

In order to claim deductions for business travel and entertainment expenses, adequate records must be kept to support such deductions.

A page of a Travel & Entertainment Log may look like:

Travel & Entertainment Log

DATE	DESTINATION	PURPOSE	MILEAGE	ACTIVITIES	COST

Payroll Register

Employers must conform with all applicable federal and state employment laws concerning minimum wages, overtime, etc. Thus, it is important to maintain a payroll system to record all pertinent payroll information.

A Payroll Register can be used to summarize and compute payroll for each payroll period, such as biweekly or monthly. A Payroll Register should include:

1. Gross earnings, including regular pay and overtime pay
2. Taxable earnings
3. Tax withholding
4. Net pay[4]
5. Paid time-off or vacation hours

---

[4] Commonly known as take-home pay.

PART II

ACCOUNTING

Chapter 6

Accounting Authorities

Financial Accounting Foundation

The Financial Accounting Foundation is an independent, non-profit organization responsible for overseeing, administrating, financing and the appointment of the Financial Accounting Standards Board (FASB) and the Governmental Accounting Standards Board (GASB). The FASB establish financial reporting and accounting standards for private and public companies as well as non-profit organizations. The GASB performs the same functions as FASB on a government level with the Federal, state and local governments.

Generally Accepted Accounting Principles

The framework of accounting rules commonly used by accountants in the preparation of financial statements is known as Generally Accepted Accounting Principles (GAAP). In the United States, GAAP is promulgated by the FASB. The goal of GAAP is to ensure that financial statements are prepared under a consistent set of accounting rules so that financial statements from different companies can be compared to each other in a meaningful way.

All publicly traded companies are required by the Securities and Exchange Commission to follow GAAP when preparing their financial statements. Governmental entities are also required to follow GAAP, but a different set of GAAP guidelines is specially reserved for government organizations. Thus, the financial statements of government entities can be quite different from those of publicly traded companies, even though both government entities and publicly traded companies are following GAAP.

The accrual method of accounting must be used in order for a business to be considered as GAAP-compliant.

International Financial Reporting Standards

International Financial Reporting Standards (IFRS) is the accounting framework used by approximately 100 countries worldwide outside the United States. IFRS is promulgated by the International Accounting Standards Board (IASB) headquartered in London. IASB is a committee of fourteen members from different countries. The biggest difference between GAAP and IFRS is that GAAP is mostly based on rules, and IFRS is mostly based on principles.

Since 2002, the IASB and FASB have been working together to achieve convergence of the IFRS and GAAP. In 2008, the two boards issued an update to the Memorandum of Understanding, which identified a series of priorities and milestones, emphasizing the goal of joint projects to produce a set of common, principle-based standards.

CHAPTER 7

FINANCIAL STATEMENTS

All the business transactions recorded through bookkeeping efforts can be used to prepare financial statements. In general, financial statements are typically used for presenting past financial information (known as actual performance statements) of a business. But they can also be used for predicting future profitability of the business (known as *pro forma* statements).

It is imperative for a business owner to understand at least the following four different financial statements:

1. Income Statement
2. Balance Sheet
3. Cash Flow Statement
4. Statement of Retained Earnings

Information from these four different financial statements can be utilized to analyze the performance of a business in order to make crucial business decisions.

Income Statement

An Income Statement[5] shows a business' financial performance over a period of time, such as a month, a quarter or a year. It shows where monies came from and where they were spent over the stated period of time. An Income Statement typically has three sections, namely, a Revenues section, an Expenses section and a Profit section. Thus, an Income Statement can be viewed as a formal presentation of the profit equation shown in Chapter 1 because its three sections correspond to the three variables of the profit equation.

For the single-entry method of bookkeeping, the sole source of the revenues and expenses information for the Revenues and Expenses sections of an Income Statement, respectively, is the Revenue & Expense Journal. The Revenue & Expense Journal provides the breakdown cost of each revenue item and each expense item, along with the corresponding totals.

For the double-entry method of bookkeeping, the revenues and expenses information for the Revenues and Expenses sections of an Income Statement, respectively, come from the Revenues accounts and the Expenses accounts. Each account of the Revenues accounts yields the cost of each revenue item. Similarly, each account of the Expenses accounts yields the cost of each expense item.

An example of an Income Statement for a Acne Company for the year 2018 is as follows:

---

[5] Also known as Profit & Loss Statement.

Income Statement

Acne Company
1/1/2018 to 12/31/2018

Revenues	
Services	$350,000
Interest	2,000
Total Revenues	352,000
Expenses	
Advertising	1,000
Office Supplies	2,000
Insurance	3,000
Rent	25,000
Salaries	60,000
Taxes	10,000
Total Expenses	101,000
Net Profit	$251,000

It is beneficial to present the items on an Income Statement with relevant groupings and subtotals.

Balance Sheet

A Balance Sheet shows a business' financial condition at a given point of time. It is typically prepared at the close of an accounting period, such as a month, a quarter or a year. If an Income Statement is like a movie, a Balance Sheet is like a photograph. A Balance Sheet shows a snapshot of what a business owns and owes at a given moment. From that, a business' financial position can be determined.

An example of a Balance Sheet for a company at the end of the year 2018 is as follows:

```
                    Balance Sheet

                    Acne Company
                  December 31, 2018


     Assets
     Cash                                    $50,000
     Accounts Receivable                      20,000
     Equipment                                 5,000
     Total Assets                             75,000

     Liabilities
     Accounts Payable                         20,000
     Loan Payable                             10,000
     Total Liabilities                        30,000

     Owner's Equity
     Capital                                  20,000
     Retained Profits                         25,000
     Total Owner's Equity                    $45,000


     Total Liabilities + Owners' Equity = $75,000
```

A Balance Sheet has three sections, namely, an Assets section, a Liabilities section, and an Owner's Equity section. Thus, a Balance Sheet can be viewed as a formal presentation of the accounting equation shown in Chapter 1 because its three sections correspond to the three variables of the accounting equation.

For the single-entry method of bookkeeping, the source of the various information summarized by the Balance Sheet is the General Records.

For the double-entry method of bookkeeping, the information for the Assets, Liabilities and Owner's Equity sections comes from the Assets, Liabilities, and Equity accounts, respectively. Each of the Assets accounts yields the value of each asset item. Similarly, each of the Liabilities accounts yields the value of each liability item, and each of the Equity accounts yields the value of each equity item.

Cash Flow Statement

A Cash Flow Statement reports a business' cash inflows and outflows over an accounting period. It shows the cash flows of the business, divided into categories according to three major activities, namely, operating, investing and financing.

For a business employing the cash method of accounting, the Cash Flow Statement serves the same purpose of an Income Statement. However, for business using the accrual method of accounting, the Income Statement reports the business' performance on an accrual basis, and the Cash Flow Statement provides a different view by reporting cash flow activities on a cash basis.

An example of a Cash Flow Statement of a company is as follows:

Cash Flow Statement

1/1/2018 to 12/31/2018

From Operating Activities

```
    Cash Inflows:
    Receipts from clients                         $300,000
    Less Accounts Receivable                       -20,000

    Cash Outflows:
    Advertising                                     -1,000
    Office Supplies                                 -2,000
    Insurance                                       -5,000
    Rent                                           -24,000
    Salaries                                       -60,000
    Taxes                                          -10,000
Net Cash Flow from Operating Activities            178,000
```

From Investing Activities
```
Purchase of Building                                10,000
Net Cash Flow from Investing Activities            -10,000
```

From Financing Activities
```
Owner's Investment                                  20,000
Loan                                                10,000
Net Cash Flow from Financing Activities             30,000

Net increase in cash                              $198,000
```

Statement of Retained Earnings

A Statement of Retained Earnings shows the changes of a business' retained earnings over a period of time. The Statement of Retained Earnings functions like a bridge between the Balance Sheet and the Income Statement.

For example, over the course of 2018, a business' profit was $50,000. In December of 2018, it paid a profit distribution of $20,000 to its owners. Its retained earnings statement for year 2018 would be as follows:

```
              Statement of Retained Earnings

Retained Earnings, 1/1/2018                    0
Profit                                    50,000
Distribution Paid to Owners              -20,000
Retained Earnings, 12/31/2018             30,000
```

Then, in 2019, the business' profit was $70,000, and it paid a $75,000 in profit distributions to its owners, its 2019 retained earnings statement would become:

```
              Statement of Retained Earnings

Retained Earnings, 1/1/2019               30,000
Profit                                    70,000
Distribution Paid to Owners              -75,000
Retained Earnings, 12/31/2019             25,000
```

The definition of retained earnings—the sum of a business' undistributed profits over the entire existence of the business—may sound as if a business' retained earnings balance must be sitting around somewhere as cash in a checking or savings account. In all likelihood, that is not the case. Just because a business has not distributed its profits to its owners does not mean it has not already used the money for something else, such as client advances, salaries, new equipment, etc.

Chapter 8

Financial Analysis

After various financial statements (from Chapter 7) of a business have been prepared, the information in the financial statements can be utilized to evaluate the health of the business. The business can be evaluated from a profitability standpoint and/or a liquidity standpoint. In addition, it is very important to manage expenses of the business by analyzing where monies are spent.

Profitability Ratios

Profitability ratios indicate how profitable a business is. Profitability ratios may include gross profit margin, return-on-assets ratio and return-on-equity ratio.

Gross Profit Margin

Gross profit margin shows the percentage of each revenue dollar remaining after expenses have been paid. Gross profit margin is calculated as follows:

$$\text{Gross Profit Margin} = \frac{\text{Profit}}{\text{Revenue}}$$

In essence, gross profit margin measures the efficiency of a business to utilize its expenses to generate profit. Basically, the higher the gross profit margin, the better for the business.

Using the revenue and profit values on the Income Statement example from Chapter 7, the gross profit margin for Acne Company for 2018 is:

$$\frac{251{,}000}{352{,}000} = 0.713$$

A gross profit margin of 0.713 means Acne Company is making about a 71.3% profit margin on the revenue. Depending on the industry, the gross profit margin of a small to medium size company should typically be in the range of 60% to 70%.

Return-on-Assets Ratio

The return-on-assets ratio[6] shows a business' profitability in comparison to the business' size (as measured by total assets). In other words, return-on-assets ratio measures the efficiency of a business' usage of its assets to generate profits. Return-on-assets ratio is calculated as follows:

$$\text{Return on Assets} = \frac{\text{Profit}}{\text{Total Assets}}$$

Using the profit value on the Income Statement example and the assets value on the

---

[6] Also known as return-on-investment ratio.

Balance Sheet example from Chapter 7, the return-on-assets ratio for Acne Company for 2018 is:

$$\frac{251,000}{75,000} = 3.35$$

A return on assets ratio of 3.35 means a 335% return on the assets investment. Needless to say, the higher the return-on-assets ratio, the better for a business.

Return-on-Equity Ratio

The return-on-equity ratio shows a business' profitability in comparison to the owner's equity. In other words, return-on-equity ratio measures the efficiency of a business' usage of its owner's money to generate profits. Return-on-equity ratio is calculated as follows:

$$\text{Return on Equity} = \frac{\text{Profit}}{\text{Owner's Equity}}$$

Using the profit value on the Income Statement example and the owner's equity value on the Balance Sheet example from Chapter 7, the return-on-equity ratio for Acne Company in 2018 is:

$$\frac{251,000}{45,000} = 5.58$$

By using gross profit margin, return-on-assets ratio and/or return-on-equity ratio, meaningful comparisons can be made between the profitability of two businesses of different sizes.

Liquidity Ratios

Liquidity ratios indicate how easy a business is able to meet its short-term financial obligations. Liquidity ratios may include current ratio, debt ratio and accounts receivable turnover ratio.

Current Ratio

The most frequently used liquidity ratio is called the current ratio, and it is calculated as follows:

$$\text{Current Ratio} = \frac{\text{Current Assets}}{\text{Current Liabilities}}$$

Using the assets and liabilities values on the Balance Sheet example from Chapter 7, the current ratio for Acne Company for 2018 is:

$$\frac{75,000}{30,000} = 2.5$$

There is no set criteria for a normal current ratio. A current ratio of 1.0 means that a business' current assets match its current liabilities. For most businesses, a current ratio of 2.0 is considered as an acceptable margin of safety because it will allow a business to lose 50% of its current assets and still be able to cover its current liabilities.

Debt Ratio

On the other hand, a business' debt ratio shows what portion of a business' assets has been financed with debt, and it is calculated as follows:

$$\text{Debt Ratio} = \frac{\text{Current Liabilities}}{\text{Current Assets}}$$

Using the assets and liabilities values on the Balance Sheet example from Chapter 7, the debt ratio for Acne Company in 2018 is:

$$\frac{30{,}000}{75{,}000} = 0.4$$

The acceptable debt ratio usually depends on the policies of creditors. Since a high debt ratio means a business is at more risk, a creditor typically will not extend credit to a business with a high debt ratio or may require a higher interest rate, more collateral, or personal guarantees from the owners of the business with a high debt ratio.

Accounts Receivable Turnover Ratio

Accounts Receivable Turnover Ratio of a business is calculated as follows:

$$\text{AR Turnover Ratio} = \frac{\text{Annual Revenues}}{\text{Average Accounts Receivable}}$$

Expense Analysis

The following is a list of the various expenses for Acne Company in 2018, and the expense items are taken from the Income Statement example from Chapter 7:

	Value	Percent
Advertising	1,000	1%
Office Supplies	2,000	2%
Insurance	5,000	5%
Rent	24,000	23%
Salaries	60,000	59%
Taxes	10,000	10%
Total Expenses	102,000	100%

For most businesses, salaries and rent are typically the top two highest expense items. It is important for a business to control expenses, but certain expenses are not controllable. For example, rent is usually set for several years.

It is also instructive to compare the expenses from different quarters and from different years to identify any sudden increase in expenses.

PART III

BUSINESS-RELATED TOPICS

Chapter 9

Business Entities

Types of business entities

There are three traditional business entity types, namely, sole proprietorship, partnership and corporation.

A *sole proprietorship* is owned by one individual who has complete control of the business, receives all incomes, and is personally responsible for all financial obligations of the business. Business revenue from a sole proprietorship is considered personal income of the owner and is taxed at the owner's personal tax rate.

A *partnership* involves at least two individuals or entities conducting a business together. Absent any partnership agreement to the contrary, each partner has the power to act on behalf of the business and to legally bind the other partner(s) without the need to inform the other partner(s) or to seek approval from the other partner(s). While the partnership is recognized as a separate legal entity from individual partners, the partners' personal assets may be used to satisfy business creditors, including debts incurred for the business by only one partner. Partners share profits and losses of the business according to the partnership agreement, and profits are taxed as personal income.

A *corporation* is a legal entity completely separate from its owners, commonly known as shareholders. A corporation, which can be privately or publicly held, is controlled by its board of directors that are in turn controlled by the owners of the corporation. Corporations must hold annual meetings and keep minutes of meetings. Most corporate profits are taxed twice, once as an income to the corporation and once as a dividend to the owners of the corporation.

For one reason or another, the above-mentioned three traditional business entities are not conducive for some businesses, at least not in their purest form. There are several other types of business entities that are more suitable for certain type of business, depending on the state where the company is registered. Amongst those are various pseudo-partnerships such as limited liability partnerships and limited liability companies, or corporate forms such as professional corporations.

A *limited liability partnership* (LLP) provides the federal tax benefits of a partnership with the liability protection for individual partners. Basically, individual partners are not personally liable for the misconduct of other partners of an LLP. An LLP is formed in a manner similar to a partnership.

A *limited liability company* (LLC) provides the federal tax benefits of a partnership with the liability protection for individual members. Basically, individual members are not personally liable for the misconduct of other members of an LLC. An LLC is formed in a manner similar to a LLP.

A *professional limited liability company* (PLLC) is a type of limited liability company that may be organized only for the purpose of rendering a specific kind of professional service such as legal, medical or accounting services.

A *professional corporation* (PC) is a corporation organized for the sole and specific purpose of rendering a professional service. As a professional service corporation, PC is also known as a professional association (PA) in some states. Professional service includes any type of personal service that requires, prior to rendering such service, the obtaining of a license, permit, certificate of registration or other legal authorization. Thus, PC can only be formed by individuals engaged in a limited number of professions such as legal, medical, accounting, etc.

It is advisable for a business owner to consult an accountant (or a business attorney) before choosing a business entity because the choice of a business entity will affect how much taxes needed to be paid and reported by the business owner.

Register the selected business entity

After a business entity has been chosen, a business owner needs to register the chosen business entity with the Secretary of State's Office. A fee is typically required for the business entity registration. If a business owner plans to use an Assumed Business Name for the business, the business owner will also need to register the Assumed Business Name with the Secretary of State's Office.

If a business owner is forming a corporation, the business owner needs to file Articles of Incorporation and Bylaws with the Secretary of State's Office. If the business owner is forming a PC or a PLLC, the business owner needs to file Articles of Organization and an Operating Agreement with the Secretary of State's Office.

Obtain an Employer Identification Number

After a business owner has registered the business entity with the Secretary of State, the business owner needs to obtain a federal Employer Identification Number (EIN) for the business entity. An EIN is also known as a Federal Tax Identification Number, which is used to identify a business entity, much like a social security number to identify a person as an individual. The business owner must have an EIN to use as a taxpayer identification number if the business owner:

    a. pay wages to at least one employee; or

    b. file pension or excise tax returns.

A business owner can apply for an EIN in many ways, the easiest of which is by applying online via the Internal Revenue Service website (irs.gov). It is a free service offered by the Internal Revenue Service, even though some service providers may charge a fee for rendering such services.

In addition, the business owner must check with the state to determine whether or not the business owner need a state tax identification or charter for the chosen business entity.

If a company has employees, the business owner must pay unemployment taxes and payroll taxes based on the number of employees and the earnings of the employees (*see* Chapter 10). There are deadlines for paying these taxes that go into effect as soon as the company starts doing business. Typically, the State Comptroller's Office will issue a state tax identification number to a business entity required to file organizational documents with the Secretary of State's Office. The state tax identification is used for all employer reporting requirements to the state.

Chapter 10

Payroll Taxes

Employers are legally responsible for collecting and paying various taxes related to payroll. For example, employers must withhold funds from their employees' wages for the payment of the employees' federal income taxes. The amount to be withheld for each employee depends on the amount of the employee's earnings and the number of exemptions the employee is allowed to claim on an income tax return. In general, an employee is entitled to one personal exemption and additional exemptions for the employee's spouse and each dependent.

Social Security and Medicare Taxes

Federal Insurance Contributions Act[7] (FICA) tax is a combination of old-age, survivors, and disability insurance[8] (OASDI) tax and hospital insurance[9] tax. Under FICA, a 7.65% tax, which includes 6.2% for OASDI and 1.45% for hospital insurance, is imposed on an employee as well as its employer.

---

[7] 26 U.S.C. § 3101 *et seq.*

[8] Commonly known as social security.

[9] Commonly known as Medicare.

For an employee, the 6.2% OASDI tax applies to the employee's wages within the OASDI wage base, which is $147,000 for 2022. The 1.45% hospital insurance tax applies to the employee's entire wages with no limit. An employer is required to withhold the above-mentioned 7.65% FICA tax from each employee's pay.

In addition to withholding the above-mentioned 7.65% FICA tax from the employee's pay, the employer must pay a matching amount of FICA tax. The employer's contribution is generally computed by multiplying the total taxable payroll by 7.65% and adding the difference between the OASDI and the taxable hospital insurance multiplied by 1.45%. The two 7.65% FICA tax contributions (*i.e.*, 7.65% from the employee and 7.65% from the employer) are reported quarterly to the Internal Revenue Service by the employer on Form 941 along with the federal income tax withholding.

Unemployment Tax

Employers are also required to pay unemployment taxes to both the federal and state government under the Federal Unemployment Tax Act (FUTA)[10] and the State Unemployment Tax Act (SUTA), respectively. For 2022, the official federal unemployment tax rate is 6.0%, and it is imposed only on the first $7,000 of each employee's earnings. State unemployment tax rates vary depending on the state, the nature of the business, and the employer's experience with unemployment. The typical state unemployment tax rate is approximately 5.4%.

As long as an employer is up to date on the state tax, the employer is allowed an automatic credit of 5.4% on federal unemployment tax rate no matter what tax rate the employer actually pays. As a result, the effective federal unemployment tax rate for the employer becomes 0.8%.

---

[10] 26 U.S.C. § 3301 *et seq.*

The following table summarizes the amounts of FICA and unemployment taxes that must be paid by employers and employees:

Type of tax	Paid by employer	Paid by employee	Tax rate
OASDI	Yes	Yes	6.20% on a wage base
hospital insurance	Yes	Yes	1.45% on all wages
federal unemployment	Yes	No	0.8% on $7,000 of wages
state unemployment	Yes	No	varies from states

CHAPTER 11

ALLOCATING PROFITS

According to the profit equation shown in Chapter 1, profits are ultimately affected by only two variables, namely, revenues and expenses. Thus, in a business having multiple business owners, allocating profits can mean allocating revenues and/or expenses.

Allocating revenues may take the form of charging an origination fee by a business owner who originates a client (or customer) against another business owner (*i.e.* a business partner) who performs work for the client. The exact amount of origination fee can be negotiable among business owners.

There are basically three approaches to allocating expenses among multiple business owners of a company:

1. divide expenses equally
2. divide expenses proportionally
3. divide expenses exactly

These three approaches can be illustrated via the following scenario. In a company having two business owners, business owner A earns revenue of $90,000 and business owner B earns a revenue of $50,000 in a given fiscal year. The total expense of the company is $20,000 in the same fiscal year.

Divide Expenses Equally

By allocating expenses equally, each of the two business owners has an expense of $20,000/2 = $10,000. Thus, the profits of each business owner can be calculated as follows:

business owner A profit = $90,000 - $10,000 = $80,000
business owner B profit = $50,000 - $10,000 = $40,000

The total company profit is $80,000 + $40,000 = $120,000.

Divide Expenses Proportionally

In some minds, a business owner who earns a higher revenue should bear a proportionally higher share of expenses than the other business owner because the higher revenue earner is likely to consume more resources (*i.e.*, expenses). Based on this premise, the expenses should be allocated proportionally among business owners according to the business owners' revenues, and the expense of each business owner can be calculated as follows:

total company revenue = $90,000 + $50,000 = $140,000
business owner A revenue percentage = $90,000/$140,000 × 100% = 64%
business owner B revenue percentage = $50,000/$140,000 × 100% = 36%

The revenue percentages are then allocated against the expenses as follows:

> total company expense = $20,000
> business owner A expense = $20,000 × 64% = $12,800
> business owner B expense = $20,000 × 36% = $7,200

Thus, the profit of each business owner becomes:

> business owner A profit = $90,000 - $12,800 = $77,200
> business owner B profit = $50,000 - $7,200 = $42,800

The total firm profit is $77,200 + $42,800 = $120,000.

Alternatively, the revenue percentages can be allocated directly against the profits, and the profit of each business owner becomes:

> total company expense = $20,000
> total company profit = $140,000 - $20,000 = $120,000
>
> business owner A profit = $120,000 × 64% = $76,800
> business owner B profit = $120,000 × 36% = $43,200

Divide Expenses Exactly

Under this approach, each expense is "precisely" tracked and allocated to each business owner exactly. This approach is also known as *cost accounting*. For example, if the expenses of business owner A total $11,507, and the expenses of business owner B total $8,493 (which makes the total company expense = $11,507 + $8,493 = $20,000), then the profit of each business owner can be calculated as follows:

business owner A profit = $90,000 - $11,507 = $78,493
business owner B profit = $50,000 - $8,493 = $41,507

The total company profit is $78,493 + $41,507 = $120,000.

	Equally	Proportionally	Exactly
owner A profit	$80,000	$77,200 or $76,800	$78,493
owner B profit	$40,000	$42,800 or $43,200	$41,507

It is clear from this example that each of the three different expense allocation methods yields different profits for the business owners, even though the total firm profit remains the same (*i.e.*, $120,000). Basically, the Divide Expenses Equally approach favors the business owner with the highest revenue. On the other hand, the Divide Expenses Proportionally approach favors the business owner with the lowest revenue. The Divide Expenses Exactly approach certainly provides the fairest results, but it is also the most tedious approach from a record-keeping standpoint. In addition, for certain type of expenses, the exact value attributable to each business owner can be quite difficult to ascertain. For example, it is relatively difficult to ascertain the exact value of staff salary attributable to each owner when multiple business owners share the same staff.

Chapter 12

Depreciation and Amortization

The concept of depreciable assets was initially introduced in Chapter 1. Basically, business expenses on depreciable assets cannot be deducted in their entirety in the year in which depreciable assets are purchased. Instead, depreciable assets have to be deducted (or depreciated) over multiple years. Depreciable assets can be *tangible assets*, such as office furniture, vehicles, business property, production machinery, etc., or *intangible assets*, such as patents, trademarks, copyrights, goodwill, etc.

Depreciation of Tangible Assets

Tangible assets needed for the production or sale of goods and services are known as *fixed assets*[11]. The costs of fixed assets include all expenditures necessary to put them in position ready for use. The process of spreading out the cost of fixed assets over multiple years is called *depreciation*.

The simplest depreciation method is the straight-line method. Using the straight-line method, the cost of a fixed asset is spread out evenly over the expected life of the fixed asset. *Residual value* or *salvage value* is the value that the fixed asset is expected to have after the planned number of years of use.

---

[11] Also known as *property, plant and equipment*.

Other GAAP-approved depreciation methods include units-of-production, declining-balance, and sum-of-the-years'-digits methods.

Depreciation is considered an operating expense of a business, and it should be recorded as an entry in a journal. For example, a Depreciation Expense entry can be made in a Fixed Assets account each year to record the corresponding depreciation of a fixed asset. In conjunction, an entry is made in an Accumulated Depreciation account, which is a contra-asset account, to offset the depreciation expense entry. Thus, at any given point, the difference of the debit balance in the Fixed Assets account and the credit balance in the Accumulated Depreciation account yields the *book value* of the fixed asset.

Book value should not be confused with market value. Market value is what the fixed asset can actually be sold for on a given date in open market. If the fixed asset is sold for more than its book value, the difference should be recorded as a gain. If the fixed asset is sold for less than its book value, the difference should be recorded as a loss.

Depreciation reduces near-term expenses and increases near-term taxes accordingly. Thus, for certain fixed assets, it may be more desirable to elect § 179 deduction if those fixed assets are listed as qualifying properties under § 179 of the Internal Revenue Code.

Amortization of Intangible Assets

The cost of an intangible asset can be spread out over several years by using a process known as *amortization*. Generally, intangible assets are amortized using the straight-line method over the shorter of the asset's expected useful life or the asset's legal life.

The expenses of a business formation can also be amortized.

Glossary

Accounting: The process of preparing and analyzing financial statements.

Accounting equation: Assets = Liabilities + Owner's Equity

Accounts payable: Monies owed by a business to its creditors for goods purchased or service received.

Accounts receivable: Monies to be received by a business in the future for goods sold or service rendered.

Accrual method of accounting: Revenues are recorded under the date goods are delivered and/or services are provided, regardless of when monies are received.

Accumulated depreciation: A contra-asset account for offsetting depreciation expense of a fixed asset.

Amortization: The process of spreading out the cost of an intangible asset over multiple years.

Assets: All properties owned by a business.

Balance sheet: A financial statement that lists assets, liabilities and owner's equity at a particular point in time.

Book value: The net value of a fixed asset after subtracting the credit balance in the accumulated depreciation account from the debit balance in the fixed assets account.

Bookkeeping: The process of recording transactions of a business.

Capital: *see* Owner's Equity.

Cash flow: The movement of cash into and out of a business.

Cash method of accounting: Revenues are recorded under the date when monies are received, and expenses are recorded under the date when monies are sent out.

Chart of accounts: A list of titles of a business' general ledger accounts.

Cost accounting: The collection, assignment and interpretation of information about costs.

Credit: A right-hand column of an account entry.

Debit: A left-hand column of an account entry.

Depreciation: The process of spreading out the cost of a fixed asset over multiple years.

Double-entry method: A method of accounting in which each transaction is recorded as debit(s) and credit(s).

Expenses: All monies spent by a business.

Fiscal year: Any twelve-month accounting period used by a business.

Fixed asset: An item purchased for use in a business that is depreciable over a fixed period of time.

Federal Insurance Contributions Act (FICA) tax: A combination of social security and Medicare taxes.

Financial Accounting Standards Board (FASB): The organization that sets the accounting standards to be followed for the preparation of financial statements. All rulings from the FASB are to be considered as GAAP.

Financial statements: The periodic reports that summarize the financial affairs of a business.

Generally Accepted Accounting Principles (GAAP): A set of standardized accounting rules used in the United States to ensure the uniform preparation of financial statements. GAAP is prescribed by various organizations such as FASB and the SEC.

General journal: A chronological listing of transactions of a business.

General ledger: The book of secondary entry for transactions of a business.

Income statement: A financial statement that shows revenues, expenses and profit of a business over a specific period of time.

Journalizing: The process of recording transactions in a general journal.

Liabilities: All debts a business currently has outstanding to creditors.

Owner's Equity: The interest of an owner in a business.

Posting: The process of transferring data from a general journal to corresponding account pages of a general ledger.

Profit & Loss statement: Another name for income statement.

Residual value: The value of an asset at the end of its useful life to a business.
Revenues: All monies earned by a business in any given period of time.

Salvage value: Another name for residual value.

Statement of Cash Flow: A financial statement that tracks cash flow of a business for a specific period of time.

Straight-line depreciation: A method of calculating depreciation expense. The cost of an asset, less its residual value, is allocated as an expense equally over its useful life.

www.ingramcontent.com/pod-product-compliance
Lightning Source LLC
Chambersburg PA
CBHW080944170526
45158CB00008B/2368